A PORTFOLIO OF

P9-DFZ-706

Unique Deck
Ideas

CREATIVE PUBLISHING international

CHANHASSEN, MINNESOTA

CONTENTS

What Makes a Deck Unique? 4

Planning 6

Evaluate 6

Anatomy of a Deck 8

Selecting Materials 10

Design 12

Design for Distinction 12

Pattern & Shape 14

Efficient Use of Enclosed Spaces 16

Fantastic Front Yard Decks 19

Widen Your Horizons with Wraparounds 20

Simple Solutions for Small Spaces 22

Decks That Rise Above the Rooftops 24

Magnificent Multilevel Decks 26

Special Features 32

Beautify with Built-ins 36

Eating & Entertaining Outdoors 42

Decks That Light Up the Night 46

A Portfolio of Unique Deck Ideas 50

Problem Solving 53

Recreational Decks 63

Increasing Living Space 73

Creating Comfort 83

Privacy 93

List of Contributors 96

WHAT MAKES A DECK UNIQUE?

A deck is one of the most useful home improvements you can make. Decks add beauty and value to your home and offer a way to expand your living area into the outdoors. Every yard presents a unique situation when you are considering where and what type of deck to build. A great deck design will make the best possible use of available outdoor space while meshing gracefully with the surroundings. The best decks all deal with unique situations and enhance the beauty and functionality of the house and landscape adjoining them.

Instead of settling for a flat, simple surface, design your deck to incorporate a large tree, boulders, shrubs, a pond or a landscaped slope. It will become the focal point for your yard. Decks provide solutions for almost every house and lot configuration—from wraparound decks that take advantage of small yards by using the space surrounding the house, to detached decks that can be located anywhere in the yard to create a private sanctuary away from the busy household and the rest of the world.

There are no ready-made solutions to creative deck design. Your house, lifestyle and family needs are unique. By studying the site and planning carefully, you can make good decisions that are the foundation of great deck ideas.

An appealing island deck is one way to fill an outlying area of the yard and make it more functional. This raised deck creates a comfortable space for sunning or just enjoying an evening outdoors.

Photo courtesy of Milt Charno and Associates, Inc., George Lyons, photographer

A smartly designed deck is divided into three separate areas to break the sharp angle of the slope. Wide, gently angled stairways link the three areas and guide the user easily along the incline.

An elevated deck extends out over a steep, rocky hillside, creating a spacious deck area with a spectacular view. A stairway winds itself around a towerlike portion on the side of the house to a small rooftop deck that resembles a crow's nest on a sailing ship.

Photo courtesy of Lindal Cedar Homes, Inc., Seattle, Washington

Photo courtesy of Lindal Cedar Homes, Inc., Seattle, Washington

Make the most of a magnificent view. This expansive two-story deck extends the length of the house and can be accessed from any area inside via numerous sets of patio doors. A shaded, more sheltered area is created by the overhang of the second-story deck.

EVALUATE

Make a map *of the features of your house and yard. Include any features that might affect how you build and use your deck. For accurate measurements use a long tape measure and hold it level and perpendicular to the house.*

Explore your options. Besides the basic square deck off the back of the house, there are many ways you can create a deck that enhances your outdoor environment tremendously. One of the benefits of building a deck is the way a deck can take an unmanageable part of a yard, such as a steep slope or rocky hillside, and make it useable. Decks can be designed to any size or shape, so they can take advantage of odd spaces that would otherwise go unused.

Some common types of decks include: decks that fill the space created by an L- or U-shaped house, where the structure already forms a partially enclosed area; wraparound decks, which create a level walkway around the house even if your yard slopes and rises; detached, or island decks, which create quiet retreats away from the hustle and bustle of the house; and multilevel decks that take advantage of large lots and are ideal for yards with varied elevations. This type of deck is often multifunctional. Each level can be

designated to an activity such as dining, entertaining, sunbathing and recreation.

You will also need to observe and evaluate the influence of environmental effects before building a deck. Study the way the sun moves across your property. A deck facing north may be too cool to provide the enjoyment it was built for if factors like these are not taken into account. Conversely, a deck that faces south may get too much sun to be enjoyed all day. The effects of snow, wind and rain are other factors to consider, as well.

To evaluate your site, create plan drawings of the building area before designing a deck. This plan should show all the details that may affect how you build and use the deck. As you create the drawings, consider how the features of the environment, house and yard influence the deck design. By taking into account these natural influences, you will be able to get the most out of your new deck.

(top left) **A sunny spot** was chosen as the perfect place for a spa on this deck. To lessen the intensity of the summer sun, an overhead arbor was added. The attractive arbor filters the sun and casts thin shadows for those who want a bit of shade.

(top right) **A raised deck off the second story** of the house creates another sitting area in the alcove beneath. Sun worshippers can enjoy the heat on the upper level, while those who desire can enjoy the shady comfort underneath.

(left) **The design of this single-level deck** follows the unusual shape of the house and creates a spectacular viewing area. The low, wide steps create a graceful transition from the house to the manicured lawn.

Planning

ANATOMY
OF A DECK

A deck has seven major structural parts: *the ledger, decking, joists, one or more beams, posts, stairway stringers and stairway treads. To create a working design plan, you must know the span limits of each part of the deck.*

Whether you are building a deck yourself or contracting with someone to do the work for you, knowing the primary elements of a deck and its basic construction will be helpful to you.

Decks can be freestanding structures, or they can be attached to the house. Elements that are integral to a deck's framing, such as built-in benches, railings and steps, should be incorporated into the original plans, if possible.

Structural elements of a deck include posts, beams, ledgers and joists. They support and distribute the weight of the deck. Because of its durability, some codes now require the use of pressure-treated wood on these parts. Check with your local building inspector for current code information in your area. The visible parts of a deck include the decking, facing, railings and stairways. Fascia boards, skirts and other trim details can be used to dress up a deck. Use redwood or cedar for these parts, which must be visually pleasing, yet strong.

Ledgers anchor an attached deck to a house. Ledgers support one end of all joists. **Concrete footings** with post anchors support the weight of the deck and hold the deck posts in place. They are made by pouring concrete into tube

forms. Local climates and building codes determine depth of footings. Post anchors should be made of galvanized steel to resist corrosion. **Posts** transfer the weight of the deck from the beams to the footings. They are attached to the post anchors with galvanized nails and to the beams with lag screws.

Beams transfer the weight of the joists and decking to the posts. **Joists** support the decking. For an attached deck, the joists are fastened at one end to the ledger, at the other end to the header joist, and they rest on the beams. The outside joists can be covered with redwood or cedar facing boards for appearance.

Decking is the main feature. Decking boards are attached to joists with galvanized screws or nails. **Railing parts** include railing posts and balusters attached to the header and outside joists, a horizontal rail and a cap. Building codes may require railings on decks 24" or more above ground level.

Decks often include a **stairway** made from a pair of stringers fastened to the deck side and a series of treads attached to stringers with metal cleats. Stairways provide access to the deck from the yard or patio and help establish traffic patterns.

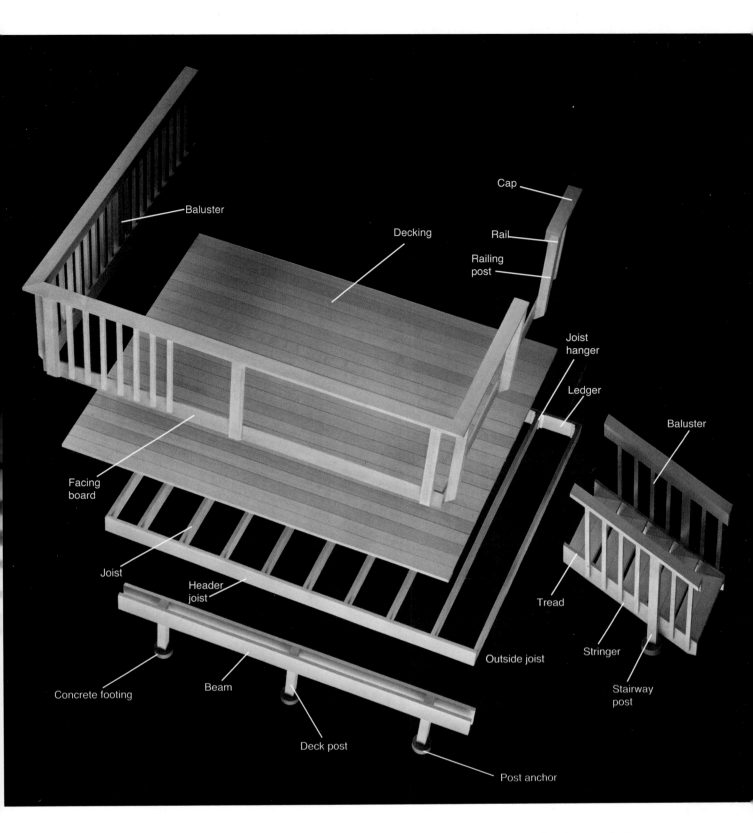

Baluster

Decking

Cap

Rail

Railing post

Joist hanger

Ledger

Baluster

Facing board

Joist

Header joist

Tread

Stringer

Outside joist

Concrete footing

Beam

Stairway post

Deck post

Post anchor

Typically decking is constructed with 2 × 4 or 2 × 6 lumber that is screwed or nailed to the joists. Beams are usually made from pairs of 2 × 8s or 2 × 10s attached to the deck posts. Vertical wood posts are supported on concrete footings or poured tubular pads.

Minimum sizes and other code issues vary from area to area; elevated decks require railings with specified spacing between the balusters. Check with your local building inspector for the specific code requirements for decks in your area.

The reddish heartwood of both redwood and cedar have natural decay resistance. The sapwood, on the other hand, is lightly colored and has less resistance to decay. Sapwood must be treated with a clear sealer-preservative if used outdoors.

The lumber used in building a deck must be resistant to rot and insect damage. The three most common types of wood used for deck construction are: redwood, cedar and pressure-treated lumber. Other woods durable enough for use outdoors include exotic hardwoods, such as Bangkirai from Indonesia and Ipe from Brazil.

Pressure-treated lumber is the strongest and least expensive choice for deck lumber. Although new, less toxic processes are being explored, the preservative most often used for decking lumber is chromated copper arsenate, identified by the label "CCA." Treated lumber is created by forcing chemical preservatives into it under high pressure. The preservative usually gives the wood a green color, which fades with time. You can stain pressure-treated wood in a variety of colors. Pressure-treated lumber is rated by the amount of chemical retained by the wood. For decks, the lumber should have a retention level of .40, approved for direct ground contact. This is sometimes signified by the code "LP 22" stamped on the wood.

Because of its durability and resistance to decay, many building codes now require that pressure-treated wood be used for the structural members of a deck. In these instances, more decorative woods, such as redwood or cedar, can still be used for the visible design elements, such as decking, stairways, facing and railings.

Redwood is an attractive and durable wood popular for use in outdoor structures. Because quality redwood is a bit expensive, using it only on the visible parts of the deck is one way to achieve high-quality results at a lower cost. Cedar is also recommended for decks. As with redwood, you can save on costs by using cedar for the visible surfaces of the deck and pressure-treated lumber for the structural members.

Be sure to follow the safety recommendations for handling treated wood. Wear gloves to help avoid splinters. Treated wood should never be burned in open fires, stoves or fireplaces. When sawing and machining treated wood, wear a dust mask. Wash work clothes separately from other household clothing.

Grade stamp for cedar lists the species, the lumber grade, the moisture content, the lumber mill number and membership association. Western red cedar (WR CDR or WRC) or incense cedar (INC) used in decks should be graded as heartwood (HEART) with a maximum moisture content of 15% (MC 15).

Grade stamp for redwood lists wood dryness, lumber grade and membership association. Redwood should be certified "KILN DRIED" or "DRY" and graded as clear redwood (CLR RWD), construction heartwood (CONST HT), merchantable heartwood (MERCH HT) or construction redwood (CONST RWD).

Grade stamp for pressure-treated lumber lists the type of preservative used and the chemical-retention level of the wood. Look for "CCA" label indicating that chromated copper arsenate is the preservative. Make sure lumber carries the label "LP 22," or "40 retention." Other information found on grade stamp includes proper exposure rating, and name and location of treating company.

(above) **For beauty and durability,** *nothing is comparable to imported hardwoods like the Tatajuba (Brazilian teak) and Ipe (Brazilian walnut) used in this dazzling decking. Surprisingly, using imported woods doesn't add that much to the overall cost because the wood is so hard, the lumber can be cut thinner, so less wood is needed.*

(left) **Exotic imported wood** *creates a unique variation of wood tones.*

Planning ahead and making decisions that include ideas for the future are the keys to designing a deck that fits your unique situation and specifications, now and in years to come.

Design
DESIGN FOR DISTINCTION

Instead of a simple rectangle attached to the back of your house, a deck can be a personalized structure of unique shape and size, custom-built specifically for the layout of your house and yard. Any basic deck plan can be modified to create a unique deck that matches your specific needs.

Patterns and shapes can be carried throughout the design elements of the deck, such as railings, balusters and stairways, to establish continuity. The design of the deck elements should complement the style of your house and blend with the surrounding landscape. For example, on a low ranch-style house, use a railing with wide, horizontal rails. On a Tudor-style home with a steep roof, choose a railing with closely spaced vertical balusters.

This well-planned deck surrounds an L-shaped pool and beautifully flows from one activity area to another. The natural stone surrounding the hot tub blends beautifully with the redwood decking.

Combining two deck design ideas *creates an effective outdoor activity area. The space created by the shape of the house is filled by the top level of the deck. A second level, elevated above uneven terrain, wraps around an extended bay window to create a separate sitting area.*

Design
PATTERN & SHAPE

Repeating patterns in the design of your deck is one way to establish a distinct style and create continuity. Patterns can be found in the style of the railings, stairways, benches and especially in the decking. Decking is a design element that helps establish an overall look and influences the effect a deck has on the outdoor environment. The decking pattern determines the spacing and layout of the joists.

Decking can be installed using a variety of board sizes and design patterns. Try experimenting with various decking patterns to determine which patterns provide the most visual appeal while still fitting with the structural and design demands of your situation.

A diagonal pattern adds visual interest to a deck. Diagonal patterns require joists that are spaced closer together than for straight patterns. A diamond-pattern deck needs blocking added to provide surface for attaching edges of decking.

Parquet patterns and some other specialty decking designs may require extra support, like double joists or extra blocking. For sturdy, flat decking, use 2 × 4 or 2 × 6" lumber. Thinner lumber is more likely to twist or cup.

*A **parquet pattern** requires double joists and blocking to provide a supporting surface for attaching the butted ends of the decking boards.*

*A **diagonal pattern** adds visual interest to a deck. Diagonal patterns require joists that are spaced closer together than for straight patterns.*

Creating a framed opening for a tree requires extra blocking between joists. Short joists are attached to blocking with joist hangers.

*A **border pattern** gives a finished look to a deck. Trim joists are used to extend the joists to help support the border decking and provide more nailing surface.*

(top left) **This feature deck,** with its beautiful starburst decking design, is a shining success. This unique deck design is the perfect solution to a problem yard that consists of a narrow space on a rocky hillside. Various areas of the deck are divided by subtle steps from one level to another. The changes in levels are indicated by obvious changes in the direction of the decking.

(top right) **A unique starburst pattern** is used in the construction of this railing. This distinctive design has a dramatic impact on the look and feel of this deck.

(bottom) **The gentle, curving edges** of this unique starburst deck design enhance the smooth flowing effect of the decking pattern. The curved bench top reflects the sweeping images found throughout this deck design.

15

This deck takes advantage of the natural alcove created by the shape of the house. The open area of yard created by this L-shaped house is enhanced with a fun, functional multilevel deck. Instead of building one large deck, this effective deck creates as much space, using less yard area by breaking the deck into two levels.

DESIGN

Efficient use of enclosed spaces

Decks that fit inside the L- or U-shaped spaces created by the layout of a house make efficient use of space that might otherwise go unused.

Decks are a natural fit within these spaces. Surrounding house walls enclose the space, creating privacy and shelter from the elements. This type of deck can be accessed from many parts of the house, expanding the practicality and efficiency of the living space.

(above) **Tucked into a tight place,** *this space-saving deck uses a unique shape, various levels and subtle changes in the directions of the decking pattern, to make the most of this small outdoor space. The separate levels create and define individual activity areas. A built-in bench also defines the edge of the deck and creates a comfortable sitting area.*

(right) **A view from inside looking out** *reflects how beautifully and efficiently this deck makes a multifunctional activity area out of a small backyard corner.*

17

A distinctive deck design *increases the usable living area in the front yard without compromising the original architectural integrity of this historic farmhouse. Instead of a steep set of steps extending from the stoop, the downward slope is broken into descending deck levels, adding interest and elegance to this outdoor area.*

Fantastic front yard decks

Although most decks are located behind or on the side of the house, it's possible to utilize the space in front of your house as well. An entry deck expands your usable outdoor space and extends an invitation to guests.

Decorative elements, such as an arbor or trellis, can be incorporated to add any needed privacy and be a part of a creative landscape design that creates a delightful deckscape in your front yard.

(below) *A friendly walkway greets guests* and guides them over a steep ravine and onto an elegant front entry deck.

Photo courtesy of Lindal Cedar Homes, Inc., Seattle, Washington

Widen your horizons with wraparounds

A wraparound deck enlarges the perceived size of a house and can be accessed from practically any part of the house. The wraparound design is ideal for a yard with limited space for a deck.

The wraparound takes up minimal yard space while creating a substantial amount of usable deck space. Rise above the grade with a slightly elevated wraparound deck. These decks can be built on level or sloping lots.

Photo courtesy of Lindal Cedar Homes, Inc., Seattle, Washington

Photo courtesy of Lindal Cedar Homes, Inc., Seattle, Washington

Accessible from all sides, this second-story wraparound creates an outdoor activity area or "yard" on a second level. The raised deck offers a spectacular view in any direction.

(left) ***A raised wraparound*** *follows the unusual shape of the house. An expanded deck area in the front of the house mirrors the slope of the dramatic peak in the roofline.*

(right) ***Fabulous and functional,*** *this wraparound deck includes large activity areas that are linked by the deck as it flows from one area to the next.*

Photo courtesy of California Redwood Association

Simple solutions for small spaces

Small spaces seem larger and more functional with the creative use of a deck to fill the space. One way decks create more space in a small area is by expanding vertically. Not only does this draw the attention upward, but it creates the illusion of space. Make sure you can access the various levels of the deck adequately. Preferably the largest level of the deck is accessed by the house.

A small side yard can provide a private spot for a smaller, more intimate deck, or it can be used for an extension of a larger deck.

A small deck is surrounded by a redwood privacy fence *and an overhead arbor to create the intimate outdoor environment that fills this small space.*

Photo courtesy of California Redwood Association

(top left, above) **Interesting use of shape, space and materials** *creates a unique deck design. The small redwood platform deck makes wise use of limited space by expanding upward using different levels to create additional activity areas. Natural stone and brick pavers are used to create a patio area on the ground level of this setting.*

Decks that rise above the rooftops

Rooftop decks take advantage of another source of unused space—a rooftop that can hold a deck. These unique spaces expand upward and offer a new vantage point never noticed before.

Rooftop areas such as the space over a garage or carport are other possible locations for a rooftop deck. They are an excellent way to provide additional outdoor living space in a cramped environment. Most rooftop decks use lightweight materials, such as vinyl or acrylics, to decrease the weight placed on the roof. If you have a suitable roof, these deck designs are ideal.

Privacy is another benefit *of a rooftop deck. This rooftop deck creates a sunny spot elevated well above everything else. Sun worshipers can enjoy themselves in total seclusion.*

Photo courtesy of Western Wood Products Association

The roof *of a glass-enclosed hot tub area is also the floor of the second-story deck. The hot tub sits in a corner, tucked under the upper deck to preserve privacy.*

Photo courtesy of Lindal Cedar Homes, Inc., Seattle, Washington

A spectacular view can be enjoyed from a deck above the rooftops. Accessed from an attic addition, this elevated deck overlooks a larger ground-level deck. Both are linked by a large stairway allowing convenient use of this small, vertical space.

Magnificent multilevel decks

Multilevel decks are the masters of outdoor space management. They can be used to tackle almost any uneven or unmanageable terrain you may encounter. By using different levels, these decks effectively break an outdoor area into separate activity areas.

Multilevel decks are ideal when you want a deck that can serve many functions. These deck designs often include a number of deck and patio areas that are linked by steps or stairways.

Multilevel decks are your best option when you want to create usable living area on a sloping property or to maximize the usable outdoor space you currently have. They provide an easy way to access different areas of the house and a way to enjoy many activities at once in your personal outdoor environment.

This sprawling multilevel deck includes a large, open level, accessible from the house, at the top of a sloping hillside. The deck design tackles the sloping yard by breaking it up with a number of platforms, or levels, linked by a series of stairways that descend gradually down the slope.

Photo courtesy of Milt Charno and Associates, Inc.

A sloping, overgrown hillside is transformed into a lush, green outdoor living area by a clever multilevel deck that winds its way around the house. Short, wide steps and small platforms are used at varying levels to cope with the uneven terrain.

(right) **Instead of one long, steep stairway,** *the incline of this slope is broken into shorter, traversing stairways linked by small open landings. As the stairs descend from the top level, users have the option of continuing downward or veering off onto another level.*

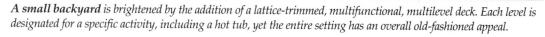

*A **small backyard** is brightened by the addition of a lattice-trimmed, multifunctional, multilevel deck. Each level is designated for a specific activity, including a hot tub, yet the entire setting has an overall old-fashioned appeal.*

A beautiful landscaped slope centers around a retaining wall filled with colorful flowers, and a meandering multilevel deck. The top level uses the design ideas mentioned earlier for filling the L- or U-shaped space created by the layout of a house. From the top, a series of short stairways leads users down the hillside, through various open levels, to a final ground level. Breaking the deck into these mini-levels creates many diverse areas for gatherings and other activities. The gradual slope of the small stairways makes it easy to access and use all areas of this deck.

(right) **When you don't have the space** to expand outward, multilevel decks make the most of the situation and expand upward. This multilevel marvel uses its unique shape and winding stairways to custom-fit into the surrounding setting.

(bottom) **Multilevel doesn't always mean a sharp vertical rise;** in this case, a large deck uses only a single step or two to differentiate between various levels. One step down the expansive deck tucks into the niche of this L-shaped house, designating another level, then descends the hillside with large, wide platform levels.

Photo courtesy of Lindal Cedar Homes, Inc., Seattle, Washington

SPECIAL FEATURES

Special features that are incorporated into decks, such as built-in benches and planters, gazebos, arbors, hot tubs, barbecues and fire pits, allow decks to take on the character of an interior room, when thoughtfully designed. The style of design used in the basic elements of the deck, such as stairways and steps, can be carried through in many of these special features.

(left) A large, custom-designed arbor was designed to give deck users relief from the heat of the sun. The open design of the structure allows cool breezes to flow freely throughout.

The special features included in the design of this deck customize it to fit the lifestyle and everyday activities of its users. One custom area of the deck features an elaborate cooking area with a gas grill and lots of counter space. Another special feature of this deck is the large outdoor spa. Situated on a raised platform, the hot tub offers users an overview of the entire setting.

Gazebos and arbors are enclosed or overhead structures that enhance a space with a romantic flavor. These elegant edifices are often accessorized with amenities such as decorative outdoor lighting, built-in benches, fountains, ponds or spas. They even contain the occasional fire pit.

Stairways create smooth transitions between levels. Railings customize a deck and create a safe restraint or at least indicate the edges of the deck. Some types of deck railings are not suitable for use by young children. Consult with local code inspectors to be sure.

Many deck designs take full advantage of the space beneath the upper levels of a deck by turning these areas into enclosed storage sheds.

This beautiful backyard comes complete with a waterfall and ceramic pond. A raised deck surrounds the waterfall and pond area so this spectacular scenery can be enjoyed by all.

(right) **This unique pedestal design** *preserves the open area under the deck and is just as sturdy as if conventional post assembly was used. The cantilevered design gives deck users the feeling of being suspended out over the hillside.*

A splash of water adds a special surprise to an outdoor setting. Always an interesting addition to a deck environment, water can turn an ordinary backyard into an amazing oasis. Other landscape settings also can provide special visual features, creating a dramatic environment.

Photos this page and opposite page, top left, courtesy of Milt Charno and Associates, Inc.

A soothing hot tub holds center stage in this area of a multipurpose deck. A small alcove features a raised level that encloses the tub on one side and makes it easily accessible from the top level.

An intricate landscape design uses natural rock formations and vegetation to soften the hard edges of this deck. The rich beauty of the wood is framed with natural colors and textures.

(top left) **The large, wide steps** used to tame this rugged terrain allow users to stop and enjoy the view along the way. The steps make this steep descent much smoother and easier to handle.

(left) **A unique combination of decking and natural stone** is used to create a dramatic, yet safe and durable, poolside play area. The subtle change in levels allows users of the pool and hot tub to take advantage of a spectacular view.

Beautify with built-ins

Built-in structures supplement patio furniture and create more open floor space for other activities. Benches can be built into wide steps or transitions between two levels of a deck. A small landing can be converted to a quiet alcove by adding a small built-in bench. Creative design ideas for built-ins can be made into delightful deck designs.

Photos courtesy of California Redwood Association

(top) **In an odd coupling,** the beauty of natural redwood is surprisingly enhanced by the smooth, clean lines of the metal railings in this unique deck design. A built-in bench is beautifully incorporated into the railing assembly.

(left) **A clever combination of colors and materials** is used to create this cozy built-in corner. The triangle shape of the seat offers more sitting area without taking up valuable deck space.

The beauty of this redwood deck can be enjoyed from the comfort of this built-in bench. An arched arbor, with an open lattice roof, is also built into this original design.

Built-in planters and planting areas are a colorful way to coordinate and accent different areas of a deck. Planters can be built into benches, steps and railings in ways that enhance the overall appearance of the area without using any valuable floor space.

Built-in planters are an excellent way to indicate a change in levels or the edge of a stairway or landing, as well as bring bright colors to the setting.

Photo courtesy of Southern Pine Council

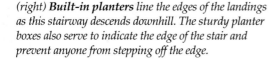

(right) ***Built-in planters*** *line the edges of the landings as this stairway descends downhill. The sturdy planter boxes also serve to indicate the edge of the stair and prevent anyone from stepping off the edge.*

Photo courtesy of Western Wood Products Association

Photo courtesy of Wolman Woodcare Products

Built up against a retaining wall, *the backs of these benches also serve as large planters. When filled with flowers and lush vegetation, this bench becomes an integral part of the landscape*

A number of basic elements, *such as the railings, stairs, benches and planters, are all interconnected within the overall design of this deck. Continuity of design flows smoothly throughout all the elements.*

(above) **A built-in planter box** adds a bright accent to the end of this bench.

(left) **The beauty of well-designed** built-in accessories is displayed in the simple elegance and flow of the benches, railings and planters.

Stacked in your favor, *an interesting alignment of deck angles allows access from three different levels onto this small platform area. Using the small edge side of the wood for the bench tops creates an interesting design effect that differentiates the benches visually from the other levels of the deck.*

When elements such as built-in benches and planters are included in the design, the transitions between levels are more interesting and functional, and they can help levels more effectively separate a deck into activity areas.

(above) **A dramatic effect is** achieved with unique materials, such as the white piping and clear Plexiglas used in this deck design. Staining the upper level a darker color defines the different levels. The clear Plexiglas railing gives deck users an unobstructed view of the entire area.

(right) **Triangle shapes** twist and turn throughout this deck design. The triangle theme is carried throughout the built-in benches and planter boxes.

(top) *An overhead arbor* and two large built-in planters create an enclosed alcove that houses a comfortable hanging hammock chair.

(left) *A traditional touch* is built into this delightful deck with the addition of this big, sturdy bench. The scalloped detail on the back gives it an old-fashioned appeal.

(right) *A day at the beach* is the theme of this sun-loving deck. A unique bench design imitates the look of seaside lounge chairs.

41

Eating & entertaining outdoors

The outdoor kitchen comes to life on a deck. Cooking outdoors has evolved from a basic barbecue to a fully operational outdoor kitchen. Anything you can think of doing in a kitchen indoors you can do out on your deck as well.

The cooking area should be located in an area of the deck convenient to the house as well as the outdoor eating areas. Also consider the needs for maintenance and storage, both temporary and seasonal, for this space.

Enjoy eating al fresco in the sun or the shade on this versatile veranda. An eating area is located just outside a set of patio doors, allowing easy access to the inside of the house. The open-weave lattice used in the overhead arbor lets a little sunlight shine through.

(both photos) **Special features are found everywhere** on this elaborately embellished deck. The various elements included in this deck design help to expand areas of activities normally relegated to the indoors and create functional areas that serve as an outdoor kitchen, bath and dining room.

SPECIAL FEATURES

Photos on both pages courtesy of California Redwood Association

(right) ***Built-in benches*** *and movable tables let you enjoy eating outdoors almost anywhere you like.*

(bottom) ***Outdoor cooking*** *is easy and accessible with this built-in cooking counter. This all-inclusive center includes everything you might need to produce culinary creations outdoors, including the kitchen sink.*

(top) **All the comforts of home** *are found on this all-inclusive deck design. The living room, or social area, features a circular fire scar surrounded by a circular built-in bench. A set of low steps leads to the next level, where a large hot tub awaits. A clever countertop establishes an eating area and bridges the gap with a handy work or serving surface.*

(right) **Whether you're roasting hot dogs** *or warming your hands, fire pits are a fun and functional way to add a special flair to a deck*

Decks that light up the night

Outdoor lighting lets you enjoy the unique beauty of a deck at night. Lighting will also expand the usefulness of a deck to include nighttime activities. Well-planned outdoor lighting focuses on the best features of the deck and leaves those you wish to conceal in the dark.

A well-designed lighting plan can shape the view and mood of any outdoor environment. With the proper lighting effects, you can make a small deck seem larger and more spacious, or an expansive deck smaller and more intimate.

Outdoor lighting fills an area with light and helps indicate where railings, steps, level changes or other possible hazards might be. It also discourages intruders by illuminating the area and eliminating shadows near the house. Lighting allows you to use the deck after dark for many activities, from relaxing to entertaining.

Many lighting techniques can be applied to an outdoor lighting scheme. The differences are in the position of the light source and whether it is aimed up, down or across a surface. Use a combination of lighting techniques to bring light to different parts of your deck and link it with the rest of your outdoor lighting.

The use of outdoor lighting helps illuminate the large upper-level deck and the extensive area underneath. Careful placement of proper types of lighting can create an effect that is quite dramatic.

(top photos) **Decorative lighting fixtures** enhance the overall appearance of a deck and give it a finished look. Proper placement of light fixtures helps to illuminate where railings, steps and level changes are.

(bottom photos) **Safety** is one of the most important reasons for including lighting in your outdoor environment. Properly planned outdoor lighting directs deck users where to go and indicates obstacles to avoid.

Downlighting is a general term that involves the lighting of an object from above and is often used to describe a number of lighting techniques, including spotlighting, accent lighting or contour lighting. Uplighting is another general term referring to lighting something from below. Shadowing, mirror lighting and silhouetting are examples of uplighting. Safety is another important reason for outdoor lighting on a deck. It directs users where to walk and allows people to feel more comfortable on the deck.

The levels of brightness should be varied in an outdoor lighting scheme. Brighter lights are used along walkways for safety, and dimmer lights, for more intimate areas.

Post lights, *like those featured on this decorative deck, are the most common type of outdoor lighting fixture. They make a strong architectural statement by helping shape the space at night, as well as providing the area with light and illuminating a pathway. The design of the posts and the light fixtures coordinates with the architectural design of the deck.*

A PORTFOLIO OF
UNIQUE DECK
IDEAS

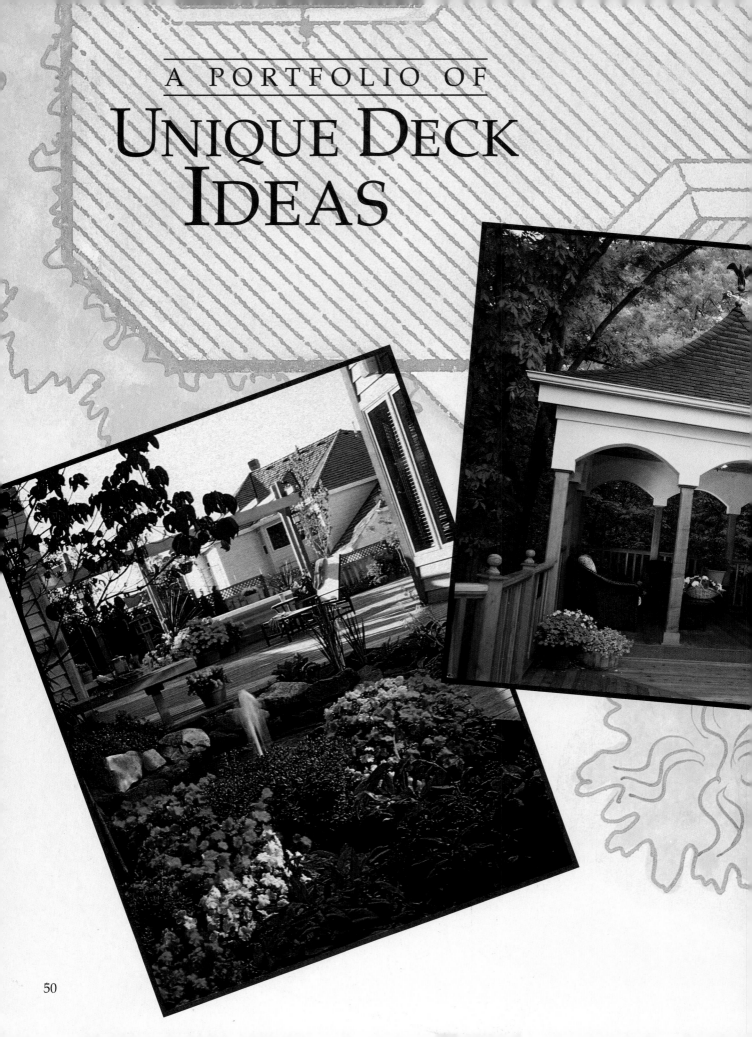

A few potted plants or well-placed yard stones can help a deck blend into its surroundings to create a more natural feeling of comfort.

Photo courtesy of Western Wood Products Association

PROBLEM SOLVING

Unique decks are designed to adapt to a particular yard or family situation while maintaining an individual personality. A good deck style can make all the difference for the home itself. Space issues are the most common problem in design, but even a tiny yard can be fully utilized and enjoyed with the right kind of deck. Huge yards can be made more beautiful, and uneven or sloping terrain can be enjoyed to the utmost. An unusually shaped deck can turn a problem space into an enjoyable nook. Best of all, deck space can expand interior rooms into pleasant outdoor living areas.

Multilevel decks offer the advantage of two or more decks in one. Upper levels provide a comfortable area near a doorway, while the lower levels hug the ground, providing easy access to the yard. Stairs link the levels and can also serve as extra seating. Higher decks have a dramatic effect as they tower above the ground.

Lower-level decks act as wide steps to the yard, while offering great relaxation areas. They can be built anywhere, from private backyard corners to front entries, and can take advantage of space away from the house. A lower-level deck is also a safe and convenient play area for children.

For people with extremely limited interior and exterior space, wraparound decks may be the key to expansion. Even small-scale wraparound decks provide walk-out space to extend living areas. In addition, these decks can serve as visual transition zones from the indoors to the yard.

(right) **This multilevel deck** *diversifies space and creates a unique area for any number of activities.*

(below) **A raised deck** *compensates for the sloping terrain and a visual gap in the house design, allowing the owners to enjoy the outdoors and improve the appearance of their house.*

Photo left courtesy of Lindal Cedar Homes, Inc., Seattle, Washington

Photo courtesy of Sticks and Stones Innovative Decks and Landscape Design

This rambling wraparound deck uses stairways and multiple levels to bridge the gap between an especially flat piece of land and an unusually designed home.

(above) **Should you build a deck** with a secluded view, or one with convenient access to fun activities? This deck does both by linking a serene platform on the lake with an unobtrusive stairway.

A wraparound deck takes full advantage of even tiny yards. If space is a concern, consider wraparounds, which hug the house profile to maximize your usable area.

Photo courtesy of Western Wood Products Association

(right) **A good stairway** *solves many problems by getting the most out of usable space, linking key areas and even providing additional seating.*

(below) **Extremely rocky** *or hilly land is simply bypassed with a well-designed deck.*

Photo courtesy of Lindal Cedar Homes, Inc., Seattle, Washington

This inconspicuous deck blends with the architectural style of the home to appear as an extension of the building, rather than a late addition to the landscape.

By incorporating the deck into yard space, rather than forcing a design upon it, you can make the deck blend into its natural surroundings.

Photo courtesy of Sticks and Stones Innovative Decks and Landscape Design

*A **large deck** will frequently come in contact with natural obstacles, like trees and boulders. Instead of removing them, why not enhance the deck by incorporating nature into the design?*

***Problem areas** like sloping yards can be solved with raised decks. This cantilevered design is as original as it is practical.*

Overhead construction emphasizes the placement of the pool and celebrates it as the central feature of this deck. With bordering benches and chairs, this majestic backyard scene is ideal for recreation and socializing.

Photo courtesy of Lindal Cedar Homes, Inc., Seattle, Washington

RECREATIONAL DECKS

For pure relaxation and enjoyment, decks are simply unbeatable. In today's world, even suburban communities are getting very crowded, and recreational space is in high demand. Luckily, large families and single homeowners alike can fully enjoy a deck if it's built to suit their recreational needs.

A large, rambling deck offers a lot of room for games, dining and socializing. Such decks are obviously well suited to active family life. Rather than limit yourself to a large, single-level deck, however, you might want to consider a linked collection of variously sized smaller decks, which lend a natural feel to almost any setting.

Waterside decks are natural settings for entertainment and recreation. Decks can frame the settings for pools, artificial and natural water sources, and hot tubs while providing nonslip walkways and convenient drainage. One of the most common deck features is the hot tub, which can be either the centerpoint of the deck or a very private spot sequestered in a corner. Swimming-pool areas are usually great deck locations. From the safety of the deck, you can enjoy the beauty of the pool and monitor the day's activities.

Decks can be so much more than simple relaxation platforms. A fire pit or barbecue surrounded by built-in benches, for example, is the ideal entertainment area. A perfect setting for outdoor parties, a well-designed deck saves you the trouble of extensive set-up, and allows you to bask in the glory of the outdoors.

Photo courtesy of California Redwood Association

Combine a fire pit with a hot tub and plenty of deck space to create a recreational hot spot. Whether gathering quietly around the fire pit with the family or entertaining a houseful of guests, you will love this deck style. Notice the benches, which are placed conveniently around the pit for great conversation.

Photo courtesy of Lindal Cedar Homes, Inc., Seattle, Washington

A high vantage point allows you to enjoy the weather while keeping tabs on the action below.

Ideal recreational decks like this one are able to support a variety of activities while maintaining a unity of style.

*A **dramatic series** of mini-decks serves as an access stairway to a beautiful pool. The main deck is covered for comfort when relaxing or cooking out.*

Photos both pages courtesy of Milt Charno and Associates, Inc., photo top right, George Lyons, photographer

(above) **This solid, waterside deck** *uses a nearby tree for occasional shade and provides elegant access to water activities day and night.*

(above) **A multilevel design** *allows several activities to take place at once without isolating any particular group.*

Photo courtesy of Milt Charno and Associates, Inc.

You may choose to design a deck for a very specific purpose. Secure railings, a private setting and good lighting are the focus points for this pool deck.

Photo courtesy of California Redwood Association

Even though this hot tub is sunk into the deck surface, it is still a very prominent visual feature of the deck design.

Following the contours of the pool, this large, sweeping deck accentuates its refreshing beauty.

Angles spread out in many directions to create the illusion of space, while steps provide additional seating. When space is limited, this angular type of deck can be the ideal solution.

Wooden pool decks *are generally favored over cement because they heat up much more slowly. Here a large deck surrounds a backyard pool, each complementing the other.*

A secluded, *shaded deck position can be a great place for a hot tub. This hot tub is positioned away from the main socializing area for increased privacy.*

Outdoor dining *is a pleasure on a well-designed deck. This bi-level celebrates the eating area by surrounding it with benches and flowers.*

Photo courtesy of Southern Pine Council

INCREASING LIVING SPACE

You can literally expand your rooms into indoor/outdoor living areas with a well-designed deck. A stationary barbecue, for example, transforms deck space into an outdoor kitchen. Since most barbecuing is done while shuttling to and from the indoor kitchen for supplies, it is important to plan the grill location carefully to make efficient use of your deck and home.

Even in small yards your living space can be increased dramatically by decks. Wraparound decks, which hug the profile of the house, are common in such areas. These designs open up interior living rooms to extend the range of usable footage. Even small-scale wraparound decks increase living space dramatically. From indoors, these decks give the visual impression of an indoor/outdoor room that extends beyond the boundaries of your home's walls and windows.

Certain features can help to make your deck a viable extension of your home. Good outdoor lighting will increase your actual time on the deck by making the area as useful at night as it is during the day. Good outdoor lighting emphasizes the beautiful aspects of the deck and de-emphasizes the undesirable characteristics.

Attractive railings and benches offer a furnished appearance and visually unify the deck with its surroundings. Additionally, wall-type railings that circle the entire deck add privacy to make the area even more a part of your home.

Finally, good storage space can transform the deck into an outdoor living area by decreasing the time spent running in and out of the house. Storage doesn't have to be obtrusive. Benches can be made to open and store lawn or cooking equipment. Cabinets can be attached to existing walls, and raised decks can have convenient storage space built underneath them. Even space under stairways, often useless for other functions, can be turned into storage areas.

(below) **The view** alone makes this deck a beauty. With the right location, nature itself becomes a brilliant element of the house.

The broad, flat features of this deck fit perfectly with the style of the home, making it seem like a true extension of the interior living space.

*A **low-lying deck** planes out from a back entrance, extending the nearest interior room well into the backyard for increased open-air enjoyment.*

Even in the dead of winter this beautiful deck seems a part of the home's basic structure. With a view like this, who wouldn't take advantage of the increased living space the deck provides?

This impressive side deck opens up the interior rooms and, with its stunning view of the countryside, encourages constant summertime use.

Photos both pages courtesy of Lindal Cedar Homes, Inc.; Seattle, Washington

Easing the transition *from indoors to outdoors, this design moves the living space from the home, to the sun room, to the deck. Such a design provides interesting variety to your home.*

Raised construction, combined with a dramatic wall of windows, draws people from the interior living space into the expanse of nature.

Huge windows encourage a feeling of openess and are themselves a beautiful feature of this wraparound deck.

Photo courtesy of California Redwood Association

Lighting fixtures allow you to take advantage of your deck space at any hour. This light is unobtrusive yet effective, helping to bring the indoors outside.

Photo courtesy of Lindal Cedar Homes, Inc., Seattle, Washington

Photo courtesy of Lindal Cedar Homes, Inc., Seattle, Washington

A good view draws people outside. Here, a small pond complements a practical deck design. Rectangular benches and planters provide a functional frame for the setting, while the nearby trees and shrubs allow the deck to blend into the landscape.

This impressive gazebo provides shelter and lends an indoor feel to an outdoor setting. With the comfortable seating and solid roof, this redwood deck setting is truly an outdoor living room.

Photo courtesy of CaddCon Designs

CREATING COMFORT

A deck is useless if you don't enjoy spending time on it. Sometimes it's the final touches or a few added features that make the deck an enjoyable outdoor living area.

Planters can ease the visual transition between the house and lawn, while framing the deck in its surroundings. Plants spilling forth from these open spaces dull the hard-edged boundaries, lending a more natural feel to the setting.

When temperatures rise or rain comes pouring down, a covered deck or a gazebo can be a blessing. But overhead deck construction can do much more than offer protection; it can celebrate the area itself. A slotted overhead construction creates interesting lighting while keeping the deck cool. Overhead structures can incorporate removable plastic screens

or vegetation, and a canopy with hanging plants draws attention upward to create the illusion of space. A gateway arbor can announce the entrance to a yard with elegant style.

A trellis is an open latticework structure for climbing plants that lends privacy and a feeling of enclosure to the deck while letting light filter in. It is important to make sure the trellis blends into the architectural design of the deck and the home to achieve visual harmony.

Gazebos are generally freestanding structures that offer a separate outdoor space while remaining an integral part of the deck structure. They offer both visual drama and physical practicality. If you want a secure feeling of enclosure while enjoying your deck, a gazebo may very well be the solution.

This hillside deck features a lap pool and curving design that blends perfectly with the surrounding vegetation and countryside.

(left) **Lush greenery** *surrounding this gazebo heightens the deck's attitude of security and comfort.*

(below) **For a feeling of enclosure** *on the deck, a gazebo may be the path to take. This gazebo is fully enclosed for all-weather enjoyment. The arbor adds to the enclosed design personality.*

Photo courtesy of Lindal Cedar Homes, Inc., Seattle, Washington

If privacy is not an issue, you may choose to place your hot tub in a more active area, where it will get the most use.

Photo courtesy of Wolman Woodcare Products

A comfortable deck should feel like a part of the home environment. This deck seems such a part of the house structure that it's nearly impossible to tell where the sun room ends and the deck begins.

Gazebos *should blend in with the architectural and environmental landscape. The gazebo featured above avoids visual isolation by meshing perfectly with its surroundings.*

(left) **This stylish and sturdy** gazebo design offers both visual drama and physical security.

(above) **In heavily wooded areas,** it may be a good idea to screen the windows on your gazebo for insect-free comfort in the summer months.

A few potted plants and throw pillows dull the sharp angles and severe lines in this creative deck.

Rushing water *lends a soothing feel to any outdoor setting. This small fountain draws the attention downward, while the simple overhead structure brings the eyes upward. In this way, a small deck appears much larger.*

91

Secure fencing doesn't need to be obtrusive. Here a large, blank wall is made more attractive by interior foliage; and the fencing itself serves as a backrest for the surrounding benches.

Photo courtesy of California Redwood Association

PRIVACY

Many decks go unused because of a lack of privacy. When designing a deck, be sure to consider neighbors, street noise, air conditioners and hedges. It's usually a good idea to build a deck on the least exposed side of your house.

Railings, fences, vegetation and arbors are all excellent ways to ensure privacy. With the proper combination of these elements, a deck can seem like a private room while still maintaining a connection with the outdoors.

By building around existing foliage, you can decrease bothersome noise and ensure visual privacy. Lattice-work stuctures with climbing vines also help to shield outside noise and probing eyes. However, remember that a deck is a natural open-air spot. The greater the closure, the less likely the deck will remain expansive, natural and enjoyable. Try to design the deck to strike a good balance between your ideas of privacy and the freedom of the outdoors.

Varying lines in this fence design are visually pleasing and help to make even this tiny corner seem larger and more secure.

Photo courtesy of TCT Landscaping

(left) **Although this whirlpool** is almost completely shut off from the outside world, the open-air environment is preserved with slatted walls and ceilings. The circular holes on the back walls are a great contrast to the linear design of the area.

Photo courtesy of California Redwood Association

Because this deck-level hot tub is sequestered behind fences in an out-of-the-way nook, the area is private and quiet.

LIST OF CONTRIBUTORS

We'd like to thank the following companies for providing the photographs used in this book:

CaddCon Designs
800-821-DECK

California Redwood Association
415-382-0662
www.calredwood.com

Deckmaster
800-869-1375
www.deckmaster.com

Lindal Cedar Homes, Inc.
800-426-0536
www.lindal.com

Milt Charno & Associates
414-475-1965

Pacific Group International
510-472-8383

Rare Earth Hardwoods
800-968-0074
www.rare-earth-hardwoods.com

Southern Pine Council
504-443-4464
www.southernpine.com

Sticks and Stones Innovative Decks
and Landscape Design
612-920-2400

TCT Landscaping
805-688-3741

Vixen Hill Manufacturing Co.
610-286-0909
www.vixenhill.com

Western Wood Products Association
503-224-3930
www.wwpa.org

Wolman Wood Care Products
800-556-7737
www.wolman.com

© Copyright 1995
Creative Publishing international, Inc.
18705 Lake Drive East
Chanhassen, Minnesota 55317
1-800-328-3895
www.creativepub.com
All rights reserved

Printed on American paper by:
Quebecor World

1 0 9 8 7 6 5

President/CEO: Michael Eleftheriou
Vice President/Publisher: Linda Ball
Vice President/Retail Sales & Marketing:
    Kevin Haas

Author: Home How-To Institute™
Creative Director: William B. Jones
Associate Creative Director: Tim Himsel
Project Director: Paul Currie
Managing Editor: Carol Harvatin
Editor: Mark Biscan
Art Directors: Ruth Eischens, Gina Seeling
Copy Editor: Janice Cauley
Vice President of Development
    Planning & Production: Jim Bindas
Production Coordinator: Laura Hokkanen
Deck diagrams: Milt Charno & Associates

Library of Congress
Cataloging-in-Publication Data
A Portfolio of Unique Deck Ideas
p. cm.

ISBN 0-86573-974-9 (softcover)
1. Decks (Architecture, Domestic) —Designs
and plans.
I. Cy DeCosse Incorporated.
TH4970.P69 1995
727'.84—dc20   95-20475
CIP

Redwood deck photos courtesy of the
California Redwood Association:
Front Cover, Back Cover (all).